YOU CHOOSE

Life in the
RAPA NUI EMPIRE

AN INTERACTIVE
ANCIENT HISTORY ADVENTURE

BY VANESSA RAMOS

Consultant:
Terry L. Hunt, PhD
Professor of Anthropology
School of Anthropology
University of Arizona, Tucson

CAPSTONE PRESS
a capstone imprint

Published by Capstone Press, an imprint of Capstone
1710 Roe Crest Drive, North Mankato, Minnesota 56003
capstonepub.com

Library of Congress Cataloging-in-Publication Data
is available on the Library of Congress website.

ISBN: 9798875216435 (hardcover)
ISBN: 9798875216404 (paperback)
ISBN: 9798875216411 (ebook PDF)

Summary: The Rapa Nui Empire thrived on a remote island in the Pacific
Ocean for hundreds of years. Its culture was known for its strong connection
to the land and sea, as well as its towering stone figures called moai. But what
was it like to live there during the height of this empire? Explore life as a child
on Rapa Nui. Try your hand as a stonemason in a moai quarry. Take part in a
dangerous competition to attain status and power among your people. YOU
CHOOSE who to be, where to go, and what to do. Will you succeed? Will you
fail? Will you even survive? It's up to you!

Editorial Credits
Editor: Chris Harbo; Designer: Bobbie Nuytten;
Media Researcher: Svetlana Zhurkin; Production Specialist: Katy LaVigne

Image Credits
Alamy: Cindy Hopkins, 29, Eric Lafforgue, 37, MJ Photography, 32, Oriol
Alamany, 18, The History Collection, 103, Universal Images Group North
America LLC/DeAgostini/W. Buss, 105; Getty Images: Allan Davey, 89,
John Elk, 72, Posnov, 52, 109, rusm, 8, 14, 48, 70, 100; Shutterstock: alextrp,
56, Andrew Bower, 69, Anton_Ivanov, 66, Antonello Proietti, 46, Ashley
Whitworth, 96, Brave Behind the Lenz, 23, Carlos Aranguiz, 59, 99, Daboost, 4,
FCG, 81, G. David Valencia, 93, Gabor Kovacs Photography, cover (bottom left),
Javiralv (stone doorway), cover, 1, JHVEPhoto, 108, lavizzara, 11, lovelypeace,
16, Nathapon Pangjai, 12, Oksana Belikova, 20, Peter Hermes Furian, 6–7,
Sergey-73, cover (middle), SL-Photography, 10

Printed and bound in China. 6276

TABLE OF CONTENTS

ABOUT YOUR ADVENTURE

YOU are living in the Rapa Nui Empire on a tiny island in the Pacific Ocean hundreds of years ago. As a member of this thriving ancient society, there are so many aspects of your community to explore. You could experience life as a child on Rapa Nui in the 1200s. Or you could be a stonemason in a quarry during the 1400s. You could also take part in a dangerous competition for power in the 1700s.

Whatever you decide, YOU CHOOSE the paths that will fulfill your destiny or seal your fate. How will you make your mark as a member of this remarkable civilization?

Turn the page to begin your adventure.

Get to Know the
RAPA NUI EMPIRE

The Rapa Nui were led by a chief or ariki (ah—REE—key). Arikis were filled with mana (mah-NAH), a special spiritual force or power.

For the Rapa Nui, something sacred, forbidden, or taboo was tapu (tah-PU).

The Rapa Nui held feasts called koro (core-OH) to celebrate many occasions.

◯ Hanga Roa

Orongo
◯

Rano Kau
Volcano
▲

Kaikai (KYE-kye) was a form of traditional storytelling that used string to create shapes and figures.

A pora (POH-ra) was a banana-shaped flotation device made from reeds.

Motu Nui

Anakena Beach

Young men competed in the Tangata Manu (tun-GAH-tah mah-NU), the Birdman Competition.

The manu tara (mah-NU tar-RAH), or sooty tern, was considered a lucky bird whose eggs were a part of the Birdman Competition.

Rano Raraku Volcano

Giant statues or figures called moai (mo—EYE) are lasting reminders of the Rapa Nui Empire.

Many moai were placed on ceremonial platforms, called ahu (ah—HU), mainly along the coast.

A toki (toe-KEY) was a small handheld tool or chisel that was used to carve moai.

SOUTH PACIFIC OCEAN

MAP KEY

 moai

 village/town

 volcano

Chapter 1

THE NAVEL OF THE WORLD

Legend says that nearly one thousand years ago a fearless Polynesian ariki—or supreme chief—decided to live on one of the most remote islands on Earth. His name was Hotu Matu'a, and he set sail from a land called Hiva in search of Rapa Nui, also known today as Easter Island. But just how did Hotu Matu'a learn about the island?

A priest and royal tattooist named Hau Maka had seen the island in a dream. In it, Hau Maka flew across the wide expanse of the Pacific Ocean. He spotted a rugged island with steep cliffs and rocky coves. He soared above its volcanic craters. At last, he saw a long stretch of white sandy shores. He named the beach

Anakena Beach

Anakena. He wondered if Hotu Matu'a could make this island a home for his people.

While the Polynesians were skilled seafarers, getting to Rapa Nui—and surviving—was no small task. Battered by the wind and sea, Hotu Matu'a led two double-hulled canoes full of people across the ocean. They carried chickens and small Polynesian rats to eat, vegetables to plant, and other goods as well. Remarkably, Hotu Matu'a eventually landed at Anakena— and the beach was just as Hau Maka had dreamed.

When viewed from above, like Hau Maka did in his dream, Rapa Nui looks like a triangle. It is only 14 miles (23 kilometers) long and 7 miles (11 km) wide! It sits nearly 2,300 miles (3,700 km) away from the coast of Chile in South America. Its nearest neighbor, Pitcairn, is still more than 1,200 miles (1,930 km) away. Rapa Nui is believed to have been known as Te Pito te Henua, or the Navel of the World. It is one of the most remote inhabited islands in the world!

Rapa Nui's roughly triangular shape is clear when viewed from space.

Oral traditions, like the legend of the arrival of Hotu Matu'a, hint at the rich histories—and mysteries—of the Rapa Nui Empire. One of the greatest mysteries is the giant stone statues called moai that remain on the island. Nearly one thousand moai exist. Some stand on ceremonial platforms called ahu. Others have sunk into the ground on the island's hillsides.

Ahu Tongariki is the largest stone platform built on Rapa Nui with fifteen impressive moai.

Much of what we know about early Rapa Nui culture and traditions comes from a combination of story, research, and science. But what was it like to live there back then? What might a day in the life of a Rapa Nui child look like? What would it be like to craft the island's huge human figures from volcanic rock? How would it feel to be a tribute participating in a dangerous competition for power? Now is your chance to find out!

To experience life as a child on Rapa Nui in the 1200s, turn to page 15.

To apprentice as a stonemason in the moai quarry during the 1400s, turn to page 49.

To participate in the Tangata Manu competition as a young tribute during the 1700s, turn to page 71.

Chapter 2

LIFE ON RAPA NUI

It's the year 1220, and life on Rapa Nui is all you've ever known. You live with your mother, father, and extended family in a thatched house that looks like an upside-down canoe. You're a curious child who usually spends time at the beach playing in the surf. You are almost always living outdoors unless it is time to sleep, or you need shelter from the wind and rain.

Inside your home, there are woven mats for sleeping, stone pillows engraved with images of birds, and baskets for food. The room is dim, and you like to jump up and see how close you come to hitting the thatches on the low-hanging ceiling.

Turn the page.

Traditional homes on Rapa Nui had thatched roofs and resembled overturned boats.

Today, your mother is making a new sleeping mat. Your family will need more spots to sleep once the baby arrives. You watch as your mother strips the bark off a thin mulberry branch. She pulls ribbons of fiber from the inner bark and rolls it against her bare thigh. Then she twists it together with pieces of her long hair. She repeats this process until she has a cord that's strong enough to tie together the long grasses and reeds for the mat.

You marvel at your mother's remarkable craftsmanship—but at the same time it doesn't surprise you. She recently made you a pora for surf-riding. The pora is shaped like a banana and is made from reeds too. You use it to stay afloat on the water.

As you stare at the pora leaning against the wall, you realize how much work it took for your mother to make it for you. It makes you want to take it down to the beach and use it right away. But then your mother asks if you would like to learn how to make cordage. The weather is perfect for surf-riding, but you've always wanted to learn her amazing skill.

To head to the beach with your pora, turn to page 18.

To learn how to make cordage, turn to page 35.

You decide to head to the beach with your pora. Your mother smiles as you struggle to lift it. She made it nearly as tall as you stand. Luckily, it weighs less than you do.

The palms sway above you as you walk toward the sparkling turquoise waters. The ocean is cool and laps at your ankles. You move into the water step by step until you are ready to climb onto the pora.

A boy rides a pora as he paddles across the water.

Once you're safely aboard, you paddle like a turtle to get a bit farther out into the sea. Then you turn the pora so it points back toward shore. You relax as the waves rock you back and forth, inching you closer to the beach. When you get within a few yards of shore, you turn around and do it all over again.

By your fourth trip back to shore, the sun is burning bright. You shield your eyes, and that's when you see a figure waving at you from the beach. Then you hear the figure call your name. It's your friend Hoa. You wonder what he's up to today. As you paddle toward the beach, you see a fisherman struggling to fish. It looks like he could use some help.

To greet your friend immediately, turn to page 20.
To stop and help the fisherman, turn to page 28.

Rapa Nui shorelines are known for great waves for surfers of all levels.

"Hoa!" you yell from the water. Hoa continues to wave furiously. You sit up on the pora and wave back. Minutes later, you find your footing on the beach and shake the water from your hair.

"What's going on?" you ask, resting your pora in the sand.

"You're not going to believe it," Hoa says, trembling with excitement. "My family is preparing for a koro!"

You have been to only a few feasts and festivals in the past, and you are curious to learn more. "Will the koro be at your house?" you ask.

"No. We're actually building a temporary big house just for the celebration," Hoa continues. "You should check it out. And we've been saving up vegetables and chickens just for the occasion."

Hoa barely pauses to take a breath. "Do you want to come see where the koro will be held?" he asks. "If not, we could also play a game with my cousins. They are here to help set up the feast."

To check on the feast preparations, turn to page 22.
To join Hoa's relatives for games, turn to page 25.

You're excited to check out the preparations for the feast. You haven't been to many.

"I'd love to see how things are coming along for the koro," you tell Hoa as you pick up your pora and run after him awkwardly.

When you arrive at Hoa's home, he shows you a new earth oven that's been added for the feast. You marvel at the mound of palm fronds and grasses that have been gathered to cover the oven and cook the food.

"This way," Hoa says. "Check out our garden."

Behind their home, you see the vegetable harvest has already begun. You peek into baskets overflowing with taro and bananas. Your stomach growls, reminding you that you haven't eaten since morning. Playing in the ocean and learning about the preparations for the feast have made you hungry.

"Now for the big reveal," Hoa announces.

Dry reeds, palm leaves, and other plant materials covered the wooden frames of traditional Rapa Nui homes.

You follow Hoa into a clearing and spot the temporary house being built for the koro. It is as long as three or four regular houses in a row! You spy Hoa's cousins tying large reeds together and using them as poles to hold up the structure. Hoa's sister is bundling grasses that will be used to form the roof.

"We should help," you tell Hoa. As you rush forward in excitement, you knock over a stack of bundled grasses.

Turn the page.

Hoa's sister immediately storms toward you. "There goes my hard work!" she yells.

You and Hoa look at one another, unsure of what to say. You try to stack the bundles of grass again, but Hoa's sister shoos you away.

Your shoulders slump after getting scolded. You can barely make eye contact with Hoa.

"Thanks for the tour," you say. "I'm sorry I got us into trouble."

Before Hoa can reply, you grab your pora and run all the way home. You had been excited to tell your mother about what you learned, but now you're worried you won't be invited to the koro because of your carelessness.

THE END

To follow another path, turn to page 13.
To learn more about the Rapa Nui Empire, turn to page 101.

"I'd like to play a game with your cousins," you tell Hoa. "As long as it's different than the one we played with them before."

The last time you played with Hoa's cousins, you had a fake battle. The battle was supposed to be harmless. But instead of throwing small stones at one another, they threw sharp obsidian points. You still have a scar to prove where you were hit hard.

Hoa leads you to where his cousins are grouped together in a circle. There are eight of them today. You are a bit nervous because you don't want to get hurt again, but you are also excited to play a new game.

"Okay, who's ready?" Hoa's oldest cousin asks. You fall silent as he begins to share the directions. He holds up a small spinning top for all of you to see. "We will have one player in the middle of the circle. The goal is to keep this top away from them. You can punch and

Turn the page.

kick at the person in the middle. If they get the top, they are safe. Then the person who last touched the top will move to the center. And we begin again."

Hoa's cousin shoulder checks you. "You'll go first," he says.

The rest of Hoa's cousins start chanting as they push you into the center of the circle. You watch their hands pass the top. As you reach for it, you feel a kick to your side. The punches and kicks keep coming, but you stay focused on the top as you fall to the ground. Then one of Hoa's older cousins taunts you while holding the top. You dust off your hands and lunge for him. As quick as a flash, you now hold the small top in your hand!

"You're in the center now," you tell Hoa's cousin. He takes your place in the center as you join the circle. The game begins again.

This time Hoa's youngest cousin manages to get the top. She's even younger than you and half your size. She covers her head as her cousins close in around her, and her body begins to shake as tears pool in her eyes. Suddenly, you find yourself in the middle of the circle again, trying to keep the punches and kicks from landing on her. You push her out of the circle and scramble behind her.

"We're done playing," you yell, holding Hoa's cousin's hand in yours.

Hoa's cousins start teasing you both. You wave them off and pick up your pora. You hold your head high as you walk home under the comfort of swaying palm trees, knowing you kept Hoa's young cousin from getting hurt.

THE END

To follow another path, turn to page 13.
To learn more about the Rapa Nui Empire, turn to page 101.

It looks like the fisherman could really use some help, so you paddle in his direction. As you do, you think of the times you've gone fishing. As a young child, you loved to slurp crabs and eat sea urchins raw. And your favorite food was sea snail. Your mother also fed you shark liver and marrow from tuna fish to make sure you had your vitamins and minerals.

You glide close to the fisherman and wave. "Hello! Do you need some help?" you ask.

"I sure do," the fisherman says. "I'm not having much luck yet." Then he holds up a fish charm made of stone. He explains that it was given to him by a priest in your village.

"Some charms are shaped like birds or decorated with fish," he says as he places the charm in a small basket for safe keeping. "Either way, I hope to catch many fish with its help."

Ancient fishhooks made of carved stone, bone, and ivory on display at a museum on Rapa Nui

Then the fisherman loads a stone fishhook with a fish the size of a sardine.

As you watch him bait the hook, you dimly remember a story about how fish don't always bite at these hooks—but you can't recall all the details. You wonder if the fisherman has heard this story too. Maybe that's why he's having trouble catching fish today. On the other hand, you may have another solution to help him.

To ask the fisherman if he remembers the story, turn to page 30.

To share your solution with the fisherman, turn to page 32.

You decide to ask the fisherman about the story. "Do you know the story about the fisherman who used stone hooks?" you say.

"Ah, yes, that's the legend of Mangai Ivi Tangata—the hook made of human bone," the fisherman replies. "In the story, a man named Ure was having trouble catching tuna with stone hooks. So, Ure prayed to the god of fishing. He was then visited by an ancestor who told him that he had to make a hook from his father's bones."

"And did he do it?" you gasp.

The fisherman nods. "But it didn't end well for Ure. Yes, the bone hook worked. He came back with large amounts of tuna every day. The other fishermen wanted to know his secret, but Ure didn't want to share it. That's when they followed Ure and fought him to the death."

"Do you have a bone hook?" you ask.

Again, the fisherman nods. "But it's not made out of my father's bones, and I am not fishing for tuna," he winks.

"Oh, I thought changing the hook might help you," you say. "But maybe I was wrong."

"Actually, you helped an old fisherman like me remember to be patient," he says with a smile. "I don't want to end up like Ure, after all!"

You realize there's not much more you can do to help the fisherman. As you turn to leave, the wind picks up and a massive wave knocks you off your pora. Luckily, your friend Hoa is nearby and helps pull you to shore.

THE END

To follow another path, turn to page 13.
To learn more about the Rapa Nui Empire, turn to page 101.

"I have an idea that might help you catch some fish," you say to the fisherman.

"Let's hear it," the fisherman replies.

"Have you seen the Pu o Hiro? The last time I went fishing with my mother, we passed the stone on the island. It has a large hole you can blow through!"

"And it makes a great trumpeting sound, right?" the fisherman asks.

"Right! My mother told me the stone can be used to call fish. She says the sound gets so loud that the ground shakes!"

Pu o Hiro is located near the town of Hanga Roa in the southwestern corner of Rapa Nui.

Pu o Hiro

You tell the fisherman about the special day your father helped you make a child-sized version of the Pu o Hiro. Then your mother gave you a piece of cord to run through the stone so you could also wear it as a necklace. You still wear it to this day. Although you don't know if it will call fish like the real Pu o Hiro, you are willing to try.

You untie the necklace from around your neck. You hold out the rock for the fisherman to see.

"This is my Pu o Hiro," you say. "Maybe we can use it to call the fish?"

You put the center of the rock to your lips and blow. Nothing happens, so you blow again. And again.

"Let me try," the fisherman says. You hand him the rock. He draws a deep breath and blows. You swear you feel your hair fly back from the force of his breath.

Turn the page.

You also feel your toes gripping the sand under the water. Is it just you, or is the ground shaking beneath your feet?

You look down and see several small fish circling your ankles.

The fisherman throws his head back and laughs. "Looks like it worked," he says as he hands back the rock. Then he thanks you for your help.

You lace the cord through the rock again and tie it around your neck. As you prepare to paddle away on your pora, you feel good about helping the fisherman. Even better, your friend Hoa is still waiting for you on the beach. You wonder what he's got planned for you. Who knows, your next adventure might be even better than your last.

THE END

To follow another path, turn to page 13.
To learn more about the Rapa Nui Empire,
turn to page 101.

"I'd love to learn how to make cordage," you tell your mother.

She pats the ground next to her, inviting you to sit. "I'm so glad," she says. "Now is a good time to learn. Especially before this baby comes."

"Can I keep the cord for myself?" you ask. It will be the first cord you've ever made after all, but you also know how much the cord is needed.

"That's a good idea," she agrees, "as long as you use it for something special."

You do have an idea about how you would like to use the cord, but your thoughts are suddenly interrupted.

"Ahhh!" your mother cries as her smile turns into a grimace. She closes her eyes and clutches her stomach.

"Are you okay?" you ask.

Turn the page.

"Yes, it's just an early contraction," your mother says as the pain fades. "The baby is getting ready to arrive, but I should still have time to teach you cordage if you want."

You're not sure what to do. Your mother seems okay with continuing the lesson. But maybe you should let her rest before the baby arrives.

To move forward with the cordage lesson, go to page 37.

To allow your mother to rest, turn to page 39.

"If you're sure you have time, I would still like to learn how to make a cord," you say as you plop down beside her.

Your mother helps you roll the fibers over your thigh, just like you saw her do earlier. The fibers are a bit scratchy, but the process is fun—mostly because you can now imagine creating string figures with a cord you create.

String figures are called kaikai. They are used for storytelling.

The Rapa Nui practiced kaikai string games with specific chants for each shape as a way to pass down their rich history and traditions.

Turn the page.

Special chants or stories are sung as a string or cord is pulled into different shapes.

"What do you plan on using the cord for?" your mother asks.

"For kaikai. Maybe you can teach me another story?" you reply.

As the hours pass, your mother teaches you several more stories and chants. Along the way, she has more contractions, and they start happening closer and closer together. By nightfall, your mother's labor begins in earnest.

As you watch other family members bustle around and get ready for the birth, you feel happy. You're glad you took time to learn about cordage from your mother, and you're excited to meet your new brother or sister.

THE END

To follow another path, turn to page 13.
To learn more about the Rapa Nui Empire,
turn to page 101.

"I think you should rest," you say to your mother. "I can learn about cordage another time."

"Perhaps you're right," your mother says, pushing the fibers on her thigh aside. As she struggles to get up, you offer her your hand. But then she doubles over in pain again. You quickly scramble out of your house and call for your father.

Soon, the whole household is in motion. Your brother is tending a fire while your grandmother gathers several flat black stones to heat. Your grandmother tells you that your mother will need these stones later.

As relatives and friends begin to gather, you crawl back into the house to see how your mother is doing. You see her squatting on the ground as your father massages her belly.

Turn the page.

You hear one of your aunts whispering about a cord cutter who will take part in cutting the baby's umbilical cord. Your aunt is concerned he won't arrive on time.

Watching everything unfold, you realize there is so much to learn about childbirth! What are those flat black stones used for? And why is the arrival of the cord cutter so important?

To learn about the flat black stones, go to page 41.
To learn about the cord cutter, turn to page 43.

Your curiosity about the flat black stones gets the best of you, so you rush out of the house to your grandmother. She instructs you to focus on heating them.

Nearly an hour after tending to the stones, you hear your aunt's voice, "The baby's arrived! It's a boy."

Your grandmother claps her hands in excitement. "Let's take this warm water inside. We will use it to wash the baby. And I will tell your aunt to get the stones."

The water is poured into a large, dried gourd called a calabash. When you enter the hut again, you see your red and screaming baby brother. Your grandmother takes him from your father's arms. She cleans him gently until his cries become whimpers and then sniffles. After the baby has quieted, attention returns to your mother.

Turn the page.

Your aunt applies the warmed flat stones on your mother's stomach to help speed her recovery. Your mother winces at the sudden heat and pressure, but then she relaxes.

You didn't realize the important role these flat black stones would play today. You are in awe of how your family has come together for your brother's birth and your mother's health. Now that you are an older sibling, you realize there's a lot more you must learn!

THE END

To follow another path, turn to page 13.
To learn more about the Rapa Nui Empire, turn to page 101.

You're really curious about the role of the cord cutter. Suddenly, you hear a commotion outside. There is a joyful chorus: "The cord cutter has arrived!"

When the cord cutter enters the house, you are surprised that he looks like everyone else in the village. He wears a simple loincloth and cloak. His gray-streaked hair is bundled in a topknot. Since his hair is long, you think he might have extra mana, or magic power.

As your family greets him warmly, your grandmother pulls you to the side. She tells you that this cord cutter was also at your and your siblings' births.

"Once the baby is here," your grandmother says, "the cord cutter will tie the navel cord in three places. This is so the baby will stay strong. Then he will cut the cord with the help of your eldest brother or sister. It depends if the baby is a boy or a girl."

Turn the page.

"How will they cut it?" you ask.

"With their teeth," your grandmother says as she pretends to bite and tear away a piece of meat from a bone.

You laugh and feel a little squeamish at the same time. You are glad you aren't one of the oldest in your family.

The baby arrives quickly. It's a boy! As the cord cutter prepares to perform the cord tying, your eldest brother is called in to help with the cutting. Your grandmother takes your hand as you look away from the action.

"In a little while, the cord cutter will reveal what he dreamed last night. His dream will tell us if the baby has good luck," your grandmother says to you. "But we also need to bury the cord and placenta."

To wait to hear about the dream, go to page 45.
To help your grandmother bury the placenta, turn to page 46.

Once the cord cutter has completed the ritual cord tying, he rises from your mother's side. He tells your brother he did well. Everyone is eager to hear about his dream.

The cord cutter moves to the center of the room and raises his arms dramatically. "I dreamed of a starry sky," he cries out.

That's it? you think. You are confused by his dream.

"Grandmother, what does his dream mean for my baby brother?" you ask.

"It's a good omen, one of the best omens. Your baby brother will have good fortune. Just like you."

THE END
To follow another path, turn to page 13.
To learn more about the Rapa Nui Empire, turn to page 101.

You decide to go bury the placenta with your grandmother. You are looking for a spot that is not easily walked over. The land where this cord will be buried is tapu, or sacred. Many people believe that if someone walks over ground that is tapu, their legs will get covered in white spots!

You dart in and out of the palm trees. You spot a small rocky outcrop with grass growing under it. You return to your grandmother and take her to the place you found.

Your grandmother nods her approval. You begin digging, and it doesn't take long for you to create a hole large enough to hold the cord and the placenta.

Your grandmother leans down and places both in the hole. She motions for you to cover it with dirt.

Your grandmother lays a stone on top of the mound of dirt. With a quiet voice she says, "May you stay strong in your country."

Then you and your grandmother head back to your home. You can't wait to hear about what the cord cutter dreamed and what his dreams might mean for your brother's future.

THE END

To follow another path, turn to page 13.
To learn more about the Rapa Nui Empire,
turn to page 101.

Chapter 3

THE MOAI QUARRY AT RANO RARAKU

"Pakeke, it is time you became an apprentice. You'll come with me to the quarry tomorrow," your father says.

It is the year 1440, and you are eighteen years old. When you were born, your parents named you Pakeke because they wanted you to be a kind person. Pakeke is also the word for the sound rocks make when you strike them together. Both meanings suit you. You were destined to become a good-hearted stonemason just like your father.

Your father works at the moai quarry at Rano Raraku. This old volcano is made from lapilli tuff, which is a soft stone used for carving. Your father has carved many moai

Turn the page.

from this material. The moai are giant statues built to honor your ancestors, and you can't wait to become part of the process!

The next morning at sunrise, you head with your father to Rano Raraku.

"I have a surprise for you," he says. He holds out a tool made from basalt. The shape reminds you of a bird's foot. "This toki is the tool you'll use for carving our great moai."

"Thank you, Father," you say. "It will be such an honor to work with you."

"When we get to Rano Raraku, you can either meet my team of men in the quarry and work on a commission we received," your father says, "or you can work with another group to move a moai we just finished."

Both options are appealing to you. You're glad you'll have the walk to come to a decision.

To work on a commissioned moai, go to page 51.
To volunteer to move a moai, turn to page 60.

"I'd like to work on the commissioned moai," you tell your father.

To get to the quarry, you must pass a plain used for a community garden. You see a man slowly laying volcanic rock row by row. The farmer waves you and your father over.

"Can you two help me lay the rest of these stones?" the farmer asks.

"I am needed at the quarry, and my son is just beginning his apprenticeship," you hear your father say.

You really want to go to the quarry to work on the commission. But this farmer is an elder who could use some help.

To stop and help the farmer, turn to page 52.
To decline and continue to the quarry, turn to page 54.

"I am happy to help," you say.

"I'm in your debt," the farmer replies.

As your father heads off to work, you study the rows of rock. You have noticed these types of rows near crops on other parts of the island. The farmer shows you how to move the rocks one by one and place them in rows.

"You see," he says, "the soil here is poor. When it rains, minerals will release from the rocks and help nourish and feed the plants."

You work together in silence for hours. Just as you are lifting the last large rock, you hear your father's voice call, "Pakeke!"

The Rapa Nui used circular rock structures to protect their gardens from bad weather and drought.

Surprised by your father's return, you lose your grip. The rock drops onto your bare foot with a thud. You howl in pain as your father and the farmer run over to you. Your father lifts the rock from your foot, and you can see your big toe is bleeding.

"Maybe you should have gone to the quarry with me after all," your father says with a wink. Then he asks if you can test your weight on your foot, but you wince the moment it touches the ground.

The farmer is deeply sorry, but he is thankful for all your hard work. You try to smile through your tears, but you know this accident just means you'll have to wait even longer before you can begin your apprenticeship.

THE END

To follow another path, turn to page 13.
To learn more about the Rapa Nui Empire, turn to page 101.

Although you love helping those in need, you politely decline. "Today is my first day at the quarry," you say. "I must continue on."

The farmer looks disappointed but says he understands. He waves goodbye as you and your father leave.

When you enter the quarry, you are in awe of how large it is. There are many moai in different stages of completion. The dull ring of stone striking stone fills the air as the men work together in harmony. Your father steers you toward a piece that has been commissioned for a loved one who has died.

"The crew and I have been at work on this commission for weeks," your father says.

"How long does a moai take to complete?" you ask.

"Well, it depends on the size. Most moai take about a year to carve if you have a crew of at least ten men like ours."

You gently touch the moai. The stone feels porous and rough like a sea sponge. Your father shows you how to use your toki to begin pulling facial features from the stone. As you begin to work on the commissioned moai with him, you imagine that you are carving one of the greatest moai ever to exist. By the end of the day, your arms are tired from the repetitive lifting and striking. But it's satisfying to see the stone take shape and to be part of this tradition.

You ask your father if it's time to return home.

"Actually," he says, "we have a bit more work to do. One of the moai is ready to be detached from the wall of the volcano. And another group needs help carving the back of a moai. Which would you like to do?"

To help detach a moai from the volcano, turn to page 56.

To help carve the back of a moai, turn to page 58.

"I'd like to help detach the moai," you say. You are curious about how the process works.

You follow your father to the upper slopes of the quarry to the moai. The moai, like the one you were working on, is flat on its back. You can see its face and body are completed.

"You see here," your father points to what looks like an entryway into the volcano wall. "We've hollowed out the area behind the moai. You can easily crawl all around it!"

"That's amazing!" you marvel.

An unfinished moai rests in a carved opening of the volcanic hillside at the Rano Raraku quarry.

"Now if you look here," he directs your gaze to the remaining area of rock beneath the moai's body. "This is called the keel. It runs the length of the moai's spine. This is the last piece of stone we chip away. After we do that, we can prepare to move the moai down the side of the volcano. Should we get started?"

You nod eagerly. You find a space among the other men, moving around the stones and dirt that are being used as supports for the moai. No one wants it to break when it's released!

The stoneworkers begin singing a working song. It creates a rhythm and pace for the work. There is a sense of community as you work together with the men in the quarry. You can't wait for the stone to break free and for the ancestor it honors to live on in the stone.

THE END

To follow another path, turn to page 13.
To learn more about the Rapa Nui Empire,
turn to page 101.

You follow your father down along the grassy slope of Rano Raraku. He explains how a moai is transported out of the quarry.

"This is one of the most dangerous parts of the process," he says. "After the moai is released, we slide it down the side of the volcano until we can stand it upright." You remember some of the abandoned statues you saw around the volcano.

"Is that why there are some statues still here?" you ask.

"Yes," he replies, "we can't finish some that crack. But for those that don't, we smooth out and carve details on their backs."

He leads you to the base of the volcano where a moai is tilted upright. Even though it's in a pit, the moai towers over you!

"After you help me with the carving, we'll move the mounds of dirt in front of the moai. Then it will be ready to move."

Rano Raraku was a quarry for about 500 years and supplied stone for most of the moai on the island.

"Wow. I can't wait to see it once it's done!"

"Then we have much work to do," your father says.

As you and your father get to work, you feel a deep sense of pride. Working together you will help finish something that will leave many generations to come in awe.

THE END

To follow another path, turn to page 13.
To learn more about the Rapa Nui Empire, turn to page 101.

"I want to volunteer to move a moai," you tell your father as you near Rano Raraku. Rather than go to the quarry, your father leads you around the base of the volcano. You see workers clearing mounds of dirt that surround a giant moai.

"It looks like you need more help," your father says to the foreman.

"You're right. Clearing the path for the moai requires as many hands as we can get but so does walking it."

"Then I'll have Pakeke help you," your father says with a smile. "This is the first day of his apprenticeship."

"What a way to begin!" the foreman says.

"What should I do to help?" you ask the foreman.

"Since you're new to this process, you can help pull the ropes when it's time to walk the moai," he says. "Or you can sing a moai walking song and keep the workers in time as they pull."

You glance over at your father, hoping he will help you with your decision. No matter what you choose, you know you want to make a good impression on the first day of your apprenticeship.

To join a group pulling the ropes to walk the moai, turn to page 62.

To join a group that sings in time to the pulling of the ropes, turn to page 64.

You decide to join a group pulling the ropes to walk the moai.

As you, your father, and the foreman approach the workers, you look up at the massive moai. Ropes are now wound across the top of its head, covering its eyes. About twelve men on both sides of the moai hold the ropes taut. Then you hear one worker shout that the ariki, or chief, is on his way.

"Why is an ariki coming?" you ask.

"The ariki's energy and power—his mana— is so great that he can make the moai walk with his blessing," your father replies.

After the ariki arrives to share his blessing, the process of walking the moai begins. You and your father join one of the rope teams. As your team pulls its ropes, the moai turns slightly and moves forward as if taking a step. When the other team pulls in the opposite direction, the moai takes another step.

You realize that with these small steps, the moai will soon be at its destination at a nearby ahu, or ceremonial platform. But first, you must get the moai down a small hill.

"Pakeke," your father says, "I must head to the ahu where the moai will be placed. Do you want to help the men move the moai down the hill or join me at the ahu?"

To help the statue walk downhill, turn to page 66.
To go with your father, turn to page 68.

"It's not what I had in mind when I volunteered to move a moai," you say, "but I would like to join a group that sings in time to the pulling of the ropes." You remember hearing the legend of walking moai. And the catchy rhythm of the song.

"Good choice," your father claps you on the back.

"Yes," the foreman adds, "then you can see just how important this song is for walking the moai."

Three groups of men now surround the moai—one team on each side of the moai and one in the back. The workers successfully cleared the mounds of dirt around the towering moai, and it is ready to walk! The group in the back keep the moai from lurching forward. The other two teams take turns pulling, and the moai begins to rock back and forth.

"Easy," the foreman yells, encouraging the men to slow down.

You realize this is your cue. You pick up a couple of rocks near your feet and start striking them together to recreate the rhythm you remember from the walking moai song. You take a deep breath and begin singing.

As you sing, the workers develop a steady pattern of pulling. The moai walks steadily as the ropes are pulled—and a legend comes to life before your very eyes! You follow the men and the moai until they reach the ahu, or ceremonial platform, where the moai will be placed. There are already five other moai in place with their backs to the sea. You can't believe a moai you helped move will help watch over the island and your people.

THE END

To follow another path, turn to page 13.
To learn more about the Rapa Nui Empire,
turn to page 101.

The workers tell you it will be tricky to get the moai downhill. Additional ropes are attached to it to help enhance its balance. When you begin helping the moai walk again, you feel the difference the hill makes. You struggle to keep it from falling forward.

Suddenly, someone shouts, "Look out!"

To your surprise, the moai lurches forward. The rope slips in your hands as the workers leap out of the way. As the moai hits the ground, the earth shudders under your feet.

You can see the moai's nose has broken.

"What will happen now?" you ask a nearby worker, shocked by this turn of events.

"We will leave it here. There's nothing we can do," he replies sadly.

This explains why some moai around the island are not on an ahu. You sit with the others in a cloud of grief.

THE END

To follow another path, turn to page 13.
To learn more about the Rapa Nui Empire, turn to page 101.

"I feel like I'll be in the way as they try to get the moai downhill," you tell your father. "I'll just go with you to the ahu. What are you going to be doing there?"

"Once the moai arrives, we will have more carving to do," your father says as you walk. "We'll remove some stone from the lower parts of the moai and flatten the base."

It doesn't take long for you and your father to reach the ahu. You're stunned by how precisely the stones were laid to form the platform.

"Getting the moai set on the ahu is quite a process, isn't it?" you say.

"It is. But once it's set," he says, "we will awaken its spirit by placing coral and obsidian on its eyes."

You always knew your father had an amazing talent. You also knew he had a lot of responsibility as a stonemason.

The moai of Ahu Ko Riku has been restored to feature coral eyes and a hatlike structure called a pukao.

But you had no idea that he was part of such an important ceremony as well. You hope the honor of awakening the moai will be passed down to you one day. For now, you can't believe just how much you've learned as an apprentice and as a son.

THE END

To follow another path, turn to page 13.
To learn more about the Rapa Nui Empire, turn to page 101.

Chapter 4

THE BIRDMAN COMPETITION

"Do you think the chief will compete or choose someone to take his place?" your sister asks.

You shrug your shoulders, unsure of what the chief, or ariki, will do. You are twenty-two years old and one of the strongest men in your clan. You are living during the early 1700s, and the Birdman Competition is all anyone can talk about—including your family. Your clan's ariki was named as one of the contestants by a priest in a ceremony you attended earlier.

The Birdman Competition is an annual test of courage and skill for power over the island and its people. You have now gathered in Orongo, the ceremonial center of the

Turn the page.

contest. You are staying in one of the many stone houses built into the slope of the Rano Kau volcano. From where you stand, you have dizzying views of the sea, including the islets of Motu Nui, Motu Iti, and Motu Kao Kao.

"The ariki must swim to Motu Nui," you say to your sister. The goal of the competition is to collect the first egg of the sooty tern, or manu tara, from the islet. The contestant must then return with the egg intact to be named Tangata Manu, the Birdman.

Sacred boulders with carved images of Birdman in Orongo overlook the three rocky islets in the distance.

Suddenly, you hear a loud commotion. You see a large feathered headdress in the distance. There's a small crowd—abuzz with excitement—forming around the ariki. Soon, you see the chief's tattooed body and yellow bark cloth cloak.

"I have selected a tribute to serve in my place for the competition," he announces as he scans the crowd. "Tokerau!"

You're shocked to hear your name called. Your sister stifles a cry. Your father is bursting with pride, but your mother is tearing up.

"Please be careful, son," she says. "You now represent the chief and our clan."

Before you can reply, your cousins grab you and lift you over their heads. They carry you a short distance through the crowd and set you down before the chief.

Turn the page.

The chief sweeps his cloak behind him as he motions you forward. "I will serve as your sponsor for the Birdman Competition," he says. "You will be the wind that carries us to victory. Are you ready to join the other contestants?"

You stare at the chief in disbelief. You feel like your tongue is tied in a giant knot that keeps you from speaking. You realize how much is at stake for you and your clan if you do not accept this honor. But you're not sure you stand a chance of winning.

To accept the ariki's challenge, go to page 75.
To refuse the ariki's challenge, turn to page 85.

The ariki locks eyes with you. You know you have no choice but to serve as the chief's tribute.

"It will be my honor," you say. The crowd roars. But you are nervous. Many people die during the challenge, and you don't want to be one of them.

"Now that you have accepted the challenge," the chief says, "I present you with these two gifts."

You nod in thanks as you accept a pora—a banana-shaped surf-riding board made of reeds—and a small woven basket that you can tie to your head. The basket is just large enough for the egg of the manu tara, which you need to win the competition.

Both gifts will come in handy. As part of the competition, you will swim a little more than a mile from Orongo to the islet of Motu Nui and back again.

Turn the page.

You're lost in thought when you hear your sister ask, "What are you going to do once the competition starts?"

"Find the quickest way to the water," you say, "maybe jump from the cliff at Orongo."

"Woah!" she exclaims. "No one's tried that before. Not from this height! Then again, you are the best diver and swimmer I know."

You're touched by your sister's confidence in you. At the same time, this is a life and death competition. This may be the last time you see your family. It makes you wonder if you should climb down the cliff face to a safer height. But you also want to win—and quickly.

To jump off the cliff from here, go to page 77.
To climb down the cliff face to a safer height, turn to page 79.

You decide to jump off the cliff from here. Even though it is far higher than any cliff you've braved before, your sister is right about your skills as a diver and swimmer.

Once the ten other competitors gather, the contest begins with a mad rush. You waste no time and run along the rim of the Rano Kau volcano until you find the most direct path to the islet of Motu Nui.

The waves below look high and black. Even though you have a pora that will help keep you afloat once you reach the water, you're beginning to have doubts. There are many rocks below, and you are not sure if you can clear them.

"This is no time to overthink it," you say. You tie the small basket the chief gave you around your wrist for now. You take a few large steps backward. Then, with a burst of speed, you run and leap off the cliff's edge.

Turn the page.

You pump your legs through the air as you look down at the rapidly approaching water below. To your relief, it looks like you'll clear the rocks.

But you are not prepared for the hard shock of the water. You hit it feet first. Your head slams backward, and your vision fills with stars. You close your eyes against the blinding pain in your head as the sea pushes you onto a rock. As you take your last breaths, you see your family's faces in your mind. You realize— too late—that you should have jumped from a much lower cliff.

THE END

To follow another path, turn to page 13.
To learn more about the Rapa Nui Empire,
turn to page 101.

"Well, I don't think you should jump from this height no matter how good of a diver you are," your mother says as she approaches you. "Be safe."

For once, you decide to listen to your mother. You tie the small basket given to you by the ariki around your head and strap the pora across your back. You run to join the other ten competitors. Once everyone has gathered, the race begins. You dash toward the cliff, slipping and sliding on the wet ground as you run. When you reach the edge, you begin climbing down the rocky cliffside. From time to time, you hear competitors scream as they fall. But you scuttle like a crab until you reach a rocky outcrop. You've now scaled more than halfway down the cliff, so you decide to jump from here.

Turn the page.

It feels like a thousand obsidian blades strike you when you hit the water. When you surface, you're stunned. Your pora is floating nearby, but you feel a pain in your arm when you swim toward it. Pushing through the pain, you pull yourself onto the pora. Then you set your sights on the island a little more than a mile away.

When you reach the islet of Motu Nui, you see birds roosting on crags in the distance. You are bone-tired and your arm is aching, but you manage to climb up a small rocky cliff. Now you must decide whether to find a cave to rest in or to search for your competitors.

To find a cave, go to page 81.
To search for competitors, turn to page 83.

The destination of the Birdman Competition, Motu Nui, is the largest and farthest of the three islets.

You decide to look for a cave to rest in. Even if you found an egg now, you wouldn't be able to carry it and swim with an injured arm.

As you make your way through the brush-covered terrain, you hear the shrill calls of the manu tara in the distance. You know their nests must be close. Still, there are no other competitors in sight, so you should have enough time to rest and heal.

Turn the page.

Eventually, you find a narrow path that leads to a small cave. You use the strap from your pora to make a simple sling for your arm. Then you lay down and hope the other contestants don't find any eggs today. As you drift off to sleep, you hope you'll still have a chance to finish the competition.

Sometime later, you awake with a start! The sound of someone crying out in victory echoes through your cave. You realize instantly that your little nap cost you the honor of winning the competition.

THE END

To follow another path, turn to page 13.
To learn more about the Rapa Nui Empire, turn to page 101.

You reach the islet of Motu Nui. To your surprise, the shoreline is completely empty.

Am I the first to arrive? you wonder. Knowing that can't be true, you decide to look for some of your fellow competitors. Wherever they are, there's certain to be manu tara nests nearby.

As you make your way through the rocky terrain, you understand why the manu tara chooses to roost here. The island is too rugged for people, which makes it safe for their eggs.

Suddenly, you catch a whiff of food in the air—chicken and root vegetables! Then you remember that in the days before the competition, rafts of supplies were sent to the islet.

You follow your nose, climbing up and over several large boulders. Soon, you spot the source of the smell. A small feast is being prepared for you and the other competitors!

Turn the page.

"Hello," you call out. It seems odd to hang out with your fellow competitors, but you are hungry.

"Join us," one of the competitors calls out. "We're having a feast while we wait for the manu tara to lay their eggs."

You gladly join the feast. As you eat and laugh with your fellow competitors, you marvel at how well you get along. But you also know this won't last. As soon as an egg gets laid, the competition will be on again.

Oh well, you think as you eat a piece of roast chicken. *I might as well enjoy this moment of peace while it lasts!*

THE END

To follow another path, turn to page 13.
To learn more about the Rapa Nui Empire, turn to page 101.

"This is an honor, but I can't accept," you reply to the ariki. "I don't think I'm strong enough to compete for you."

Before the ariki can reply, you hear your name called once again. "Tokerau, let's go!"

You look away and see ten other competitors from different clans running toward you.

"Too late, Tokerau," the chief says with a laugh. "The competition has already begun!"

"Hurry," the contestants yell as they rush past you toward the edge of the cliff. You quickly strap a pora across your back. This banana-shaped surf-riding board is made from reeds. It will help keep you afloat once you reach the water. Then you will need to swim a little more than a mile from Orongo to the islet of Motu Nui. You also tie a small basket that will be used to hold the egg to your forehead. You hope it will stay in place.

Turn the page.

You dash after the other competitors. Suddenly, they start hurling rocks at one another. You take cover behind a large boulder. When the competitors run out of rocks, they begin hand-to-hand combat. Cries fill the air as they battle one another to the cliff's edge.

As you watch, you spot your old friend Tepano hiding near the base of a large palm tree. He is also competing. The two of you exchange glances and decide it's safe to move forward. Together, you dash across a clearing to a rocky outcrop near the edge of the cliff.

That's when you trip! A searing pain cuts through your leg as you fly into Tepano and land with a loud thud.

Your first thought is to check on your leg. But you're also worried Tepano might be hurt.

To check the damage to your leg, go to page 87.
To check on Tepano, turn to page 91.

You look down at your leg. Blood is running down it like a small river.

"Let me go get help," Tepano says as he dusts himself off. "We are close enough to the village that it will not take much time."

It's a kind offer from Tepano, but you both want to have a chance to claim the egg for the Birdman Competition. Then again, you're not sure if it's a good idea to continue with this injury. Maybe you should accept his help.

To continue the competition, turn to page 88.
To accept Tepano's help, turn to page 90.

"Let's just keep going," you tell Tepano. "A little cut is the least of my worries."

"Very well," Tepano replies. "But let me do something before we go."

Tepano runs back to his hiding place by the palm tree and returns with a leaf. He ties the leaf around your leg with a piece of cordage to make a bandage.

"Thank you," you say. Then the two of you start climbing down the cliff. Far below, you can see the other competitors already in the water and battling the waves.

As you continue down the cliff, your fingers ache. Finally, you get close enough to the water to jump in. But your leg has not stopped aching, and you have underestimated the amount of bleeding. When you hit the water, the leaf bandage drifts away. As red plumes bloom in the water, you hope there aren't any sharks nearby.

great white shark

You know you need to move fast, so you jump on your pora and paddle furiously. But as a large wave hits, you are pulled underwater. Then the pain in your leg spikes.

When you look to see what happened, your fears are confirmed. A shark has clamped its jaws onto your leg. Instantly, you realize you'll never know the outcome of the competition.

THE END

To follow another path, turn to page 13.
To learn more about the Rapa Nui Empire,
turn to page 101.

"I think help is a good idea," you say to Tepano. "This cut is pretty bad, and I need to stop the bleeding."

Wasting no time, Tepano runs back toward the village. You take deep breaths in and exhale slowly out. You look up at the clouds—anything to keep the focus off your leg.

Tepano returns with a small crowd of people, including your mother, father, sister, and a priest. The priest takes one look at your leg and tells you the cut is too deep for you to keep going.

Luckily, they've brought a reed mat to carry you back to the village. You are disappointed that you will have to forfeit the competition. But you wish Tepano luck and thank him for helping you.

THE END

To follow another path, turn to page 13.
To learn more about the Rapa Nui Empire,
turn to page 101.

Even though your leg hurts, you decide to check on your friend.

"Are you okay?" you ask.

"I thought I avoided fighting with the other contestants," Tepano laughs.

"Sorry," you reply, "I tripped. But it looks like I got the worst of it." You point at a shallow cut across your thigh.

"Looks like you'll live though," Tepano says.

"I hope so," you reply, "but we should get going."

You decide to work together to get down the face of the cliff. The first part down is easier than you would have thought. Soon, you are standing next to Tepano on a rocky outcrop.

Turn the page.

"We should jump," you say as you look down at the raging waves below. "But I'll go first. Then you can decide if you want to jump from here too."

Before Tepano can object, you leap into the water. When you break the surface, you swing your pora around and climb aboard to float in the water. Then you wave up at Tepano.

When Tepano leaps, his fear is clearly written across his face. But when he rises out of the water, he has a look of excitement.

"Let's do this!" he shouts.

Once he's on his pora, the two of you paddle toward the islet. The waves are rough and high, but you cross the mile-long stretch. When you arrive at the islet, there isn't a clear place to land. The shoreline is rocky, and the land is green and denser than on the big island.

Manu tara, a sooty tern's name in the Rapa Nui language, means "luck bird."

As Tepano scrambles onto shore behind you, you scan the area for bird nests. Your eyes dart quickly around the island. In the distance you see a bird take flight. You mark the area in your mind's eye, hoping Tepano didn't see it. You wonder if you should run straight there or try to throw Tepano off your trail.

To run straight for the bird's nest, turn to page 94.
To throw Tepano off your trail, turn to page 95.

You decide to head straight for the area where the bird flew up. You're sure a nest must be in that area.

As you near the area, you spot the nest.

What luck! you think, scooping up the nest. Then you feel strong hands grasping at you, trying to overtake you. The nest slips from your wet grip and its eggs crack and smear across the ground. You turn around expecting to see Tepano, but to your surprise it's another competitor.

"I can't believe it!" you mutter to yourself. Now you must keep searching for another egg. Otherwise, this game is over.

THE END

To follow another path, turn to page 13.
To learn more about the Rapa Nui Empire, turn to page 101.

Although Tepano is your friend, you want to win this competition for your clan and family. You decide misdirection is the key.

You head away from the area where you saw the bird fly—intending to eventually circle back to it. As you stumble through the low brush and crawl over large boulders, you pretend to look for nests.

By chance, you shoo away a bird and spot a large white egg with black speckles. You can't believe your luck and grab the egg with both hands. You don't think anyone saw you, so you reverse course and head back to the shoreline.

But now you need to make a decision. Do you take the time to secure the egg in your basket headpiece? Or do you announce that you have found an egg to your competitors?

To secure the egg in your headpiece, turn to page 96.

To announce you found an egg, turn to page 98.

You decide the safest choice is to secure the egg in your headpiece first. You take the egg into a nearby cave where you can do so secretly. You untie the basket headpiece on your forehead and place the egg gently inside. Then you put the headpiece back on.

You peer outside of the cave to make sure there aren't any other competitors nearby. Then you exit the cave quickly and run toward the shoreline.

A sooty tern tends to an egg in its nest.

As soon as you get to your pora, you'll announce you have found an egg. But as you gain speed, your headpiece drops in front of your eyes. You lose your balance and trip over a tree root.

As you fall, you rip off the headpiece and hold it overhead to protect it. But the headpiece still smacks the ground and the egg cracks. With yolk dripping down your hand and arm, you collapse in defeat.

THE END

To follow another path, turn to page 13.
To learn more about the Rapa Nui Empire,
turn to page 101.

You leap to the nearest rock and yell, "Shave your head!"

This saying has been an important part of the competition for as long as you can remember. Once you present the ariki with the egg, he will be sent into isolation. His head will be shaved as he transforms into the Birdman for the year.

Wasting no time, you place the egg in the basket tied across your forehead. Then you run to your pora and leap into the waves. With the egg stowed in the basket, your energy is renewed. You cover the distance between the islet and the big island with ease.

When you arrive at the base of the cliff, you begin to climb. Your leg is still sore from your fall earlier, but you slowly crawl upward. When you reach the top of the cliff, your fingertips are bleeding. But you manage to drag your body over the edge and stumble to your feet.

Birdman petroglyph

Above the raging sea, you hear the cheers of your clan. You have won the competition! Relief floods your body as a crowd carries you on their shoulders. Tonight, you will feast like a chief!

THE END

To follow another path, turn to page 13.
To learn more about the Rapa Nui Empire, turn to page 101.

Chapter 5

THE END OF AN EMPIRE?

The Rapa Nui Empire thrived from the 1200s through the early 1700s. But in 1722, Dutch explorer Jacob Roggeveen landed on the island of Rapa Nui. The date of his arrival happened to be Easter Sunday that year, which is why the island is also known as Easter Island.

When Roggeveen arrived, he estimated about 3,000 people lived on Rapa Nui. His arrival, however, resulted in violence and marked the beginning of the end of the Rapa Nui Empire. The island's population was soon decimated by disease and the slave trade.

When Captain James Cook arrived on the island in 1774, he recorded that there was little to eat on Rapa Nui. He also noted that the islanders were welcoming but appeared sick. By 1877—just 150 years after Roggeveen landed—only about 111 Rapa Nui people remained. Those living on the island today are descendants of these people.

Although misfortune and misery persisted, the Rapa Nui people fought back over the next hundred years. During the early 1900s, they rebelled against a cruel landowner who forced the islanders to live in the town of Hanga Roa while the rest of the island was used for sheep and later a farm. They wanted their independence but didn't get it.

However, in 1914, Katherine Routledge visited Rapa Nui. She wrote about her expedition in a book called *The Mystery of Easter Island.*

Juan Tepano sitting next to a broken moai

Juan Tepano, a Rapa Nui leader, served as Routledge's translator. Together they gathered stories from the islanders, including accounts of daily life and the Birdman Competition. While Routledge's book didn't result in immediate change for the islanders, they now had even more of the world's attention.

Eventually, the Chilean government replaced the sheep ranchers with the Navy in 1954. But it wasn't until 1966 that the Rapa Nui people were finally granted full citizenship in Chile.

In 1995, Rapa Nui became the first Pacific Island to be registered as a World Heritage site. People continued to come from far and wide to see the moai. About fifty moai have been restored by archaeologists and investors. It's evident the moai continue to captivate our imaginations. They symbolize the great things we can build if we work together. They remind us of the importance of honoring those who came before us and finding strength in a sense of community. They remain a gateway into the rich world and culture of the people of Rapa Nui, and the lessons we have yet to learn from them.

Today, efforts are being made to recover Rapa Nui's ancestral heritage through a revival of cultural traditions, including dance, song, and games like kaikai. There is also an effort to revive the Rapa Nui language. Part of its loss was a result of trying to survive colonization as well as globalization and capitalism.

People taking part in a race during the two-week Tapati Rapa Nui Festival held each February

In addition to the people of Rapa Nui representing and celebrating their own culture going forward, they are driven to support conservation. Hotu Matu'a succeeded in making this island a home for his people. They survived against all odds and are thriving today.

TIMELINE OF THE RAPA NUI EMPIRE

1200s—Polynesians settle the island of Rapa Nui.

1400–1600—Peak production of moai carving and transportation.

1550–1650—Lithic, or rock, gardening is widely used on Rapa Nui.

1722—Dutch Captain Jacob Roggeveen arrives and names Rapa Nui "Easter Island;" Europeans also unknowingly introduce diseases to the island.

1770—Spanish explorers arrive and claim Rapa Nui for Spain.

1774—British explorer Captain James Cook visits Rapa Nui.

1860s—The people of Rapa Nui are enslaved and taken to Peru; smallpox nearly eradicates the population when slave raiders are forced to return people to the island.

1888—The Agreement of Wills is signed, and Rapa Nui becomes part of Chile.

1903–1953—The island is used to raise sheep and islanders are forced to work on ranches.

1914—Katherine Routledge works with Juan Tepano to gather information about the customs and beliefs of the Rapa Nui.

1966—The Rapa Nui islanders are granted full Chilean citizenship.

1995—Easter Island becomes a UNESCO World Heritage site.

2023—A new moai is discovered at Rano Raraku volcano.

MORE ABOUT THE RAPA NUI EMPIRE

》》 During the winter months, fishing was not allowed by anyone other than the chief or his warriors. Only the royal canoe could be used for fishing during that time. Anyone caught breaking this rule could be severely punished, even with death! Tapu, or taboos, like these established what was sacred, forbidden, or both on Rapa Nui.

》》 Tattooing was common on several Polynesian islands. Tattoos could communicate a person's social status, rank, clan, and achievements or spiritual beliefs. Tattoo design and placement also depended on whether a person was male or female. Tattooing was done using needles, often made from fish or bird bones, that were dipped in natural dye.

》》 Rongorongo is a written language invented on Rapa Nui before European arrival. Glyphs—carvings of animals, plants, shapes, and figures—make up the script found on tablets. Only a couple dozen artifacts remain today. To this day, no one is able to read or understand rongorongo.

》》 The sweet potato was an important crop and staple food on Rapa Nui. Sweet potatoes were first cultivated in Peru as early as 2500 BCE! So how did sweet potatoes arrive in Polynesia? Researchers believe that the sweet potato may have been brought to the islands by Polynesian seafarers who reached South America. Recent DNA research supports the link between Polynesia, most likely the Marquesas, and South America.

THE RAPA NUI EMPIRE TODAY

In 2023, a new moai was discovered! It was found in the crater lake at the tip of the Rano Raraku volcano. The lake bed has been drying for several years. As a result, scientists were able to search for new artifacts as they worked to restore the marshland.

Te Tokanga

The new moai is a little over 5 feet (1.52 meters) tall—just a little less than half the size of an average moai. And it is way smaller than Te Tokanga, which is over 70 feet (21.34 m) tall and remains in the moai quarry at Rano Raraku. The new moai has a full body but most of its features have eroded.

Moai are placed in many different spots around the island. Recently, researchers looked for a connection between 93 ahu, the platforms for moai, and natural resources on the island. And they found one! Wherever there was fresh and drinkable water, they found ahu.

The placement and size of moai there may have even shown how much drinkable water was available. Lots of water? A giant moai. No moai or ahu? No water. While not everyone supports this theory, it does hint at how generations of people may have shared a resource as important as water.

Ahu Nau Nau

Today, the Rapa Nui are still working together to conserve the island's resources, and the connection between past and present, symbolized by the moai, also remains.

GLOSSARY

apprentice (uh-PREN-tiss)—someone who learns a trade by working with a skilled person

basalt (buh-SALT)—a hard, dark rock made from cooled lava

colonization (kah-luh-nih-ZAY-shuhn)—the settlement of territory by people from another country and the control by that country

commission (kuh-MI-shun)—a piece of artwork that is ordered and created for someone

conservation (kon-sur-VAY-shuhn)—the wise use of natural resources to protect them from loss or being used up

contraction (kuhn-TRAK-shun)—a tightening of abdominal muscles during labor

islet (EYE-let)—a little island

obsidian (uhb-SID-ee-uhn)—a dark glasslike rock formed by cooling volcanic lava

oral tradition (OR-uhl truh-DISH-uhn)—stories and beliefs people share by talking to each other and telling stories

placenta (pluh-SEN-tuh)—an organ that connects an unborn child to its mother's body

Polynesian (pall-ee-NEE-zhun)—a person or language from the Pacific Islands of Polynesia

tribute (TRIB-yoot)—someone who has been selected to participate in an event

umbilical cord (uhm-BIL-uh-kuhl KORD)—the tube that connects an unborn baby to its mother's body and through which it gets oxygen and food

READ MORE

Bradshaw, Eleanor. *20 Things You Didn't Know About Easter Island*. Buffalo, NY: PowerKids Press, 2024.

Newbauer, Heidi. *Statues of Easter Island*. Mankato, MN: Creative Education, 2025.

Spanier, Kristine. *Easter Island*. Minneapolis: Jump!, Inc., 2022.

INTERNET SITES

Britannica Kids: Easter Island
kids.britannica.com/students/article/Easter-Island/274109

National Geographic: Walking with Giants: How the Easter Island Moai Moved
youtube.com/watch?v=J5YR0uqPAI8

Smithsonian Channel: Could You Survive the Birdman Competition
youtube.com/watch?v=VCjLuDlBYpw

ABOUT THE AUTHOR

Vanessa Ramos was born in Texas and raised in Minnesota. She has dreamt about being many things: an astronomer, a paranormal investigator, a museum educator, an art historian, a curiosities curator, a paleontologist, and even an actress, but a writer is what she became. She holds an MFA in Creative Writing and an MA in Education from Hamline University. She has received awards, fellowships, and grants in support of her writing from the Texas Institute of Letters and The University of Texas, The Loft Literary Center and The Playwrights' Center in Minneapolis, and the Minnesota State Arts Board. She lives and teaches in the Twin Cities.

BOOKS IN THIS SERIES

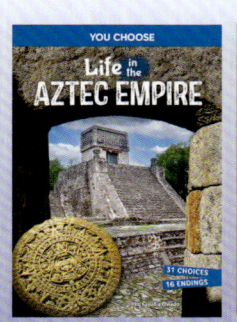
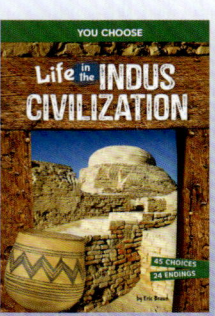
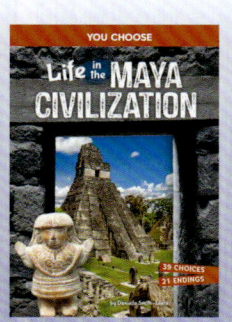